DAVIDSON
1795

D1263570

THE WRIT OF HABEAS CORPUS

The Right to Have Your Day in Court

Phillip Margulies

The Rosen Publishing Group, Inc., New York

To the American Constitution

Published in 2006 by The Rosen Publishing Group, Inc.
29 East 21st Street, New York, NY 10010

Copyright © 2006 by The Rosen Publishing Group, Inc.

First Edition

Library of Congress Cataloging-in-Publication Data

Margulies, Phillip, 1952–
The writ of habeas corpus: the right to have your day in court/Phillip Margulies.—1st ed.
    p. cm.–(The Library of American laws and legal principles)
Includes bibliographical references and index.
ISBN 1-4042-0452-0 (library binding)
1. Habeas corpus–United States. I. Title. II. Series.

KF9011.M37 2006
347.73'5–dc22
2005000924

Manufactured in the United States of America

On the cover: The main entrance of the United States Supreme Court building faces the U.S. Capitol in Washington, D.C. The marble statue on the right side of the entrance represents Authority of Law and was carved by James Earle Fraser. The male figure holds a sword and a tablet, on which is written the Latin word *Lex*, meaning "law."

CONTENTS

INTRODUCTION

It's possible that we overuse the word "freedom." Our politicians use it when they're running for office. We all use it on the Fourth of July when flags and fireworks are on display. It comes up particularly often when the country is at war—no matter what the war is really about, we're told the enemy is the enemy of freedom. Sometimes it seems as if "freedom" is just a pleasant, empty word.

There is one situation, though, in which the word "freedom" takes on a very practical meaning. Freedom is real to anyone who has ever been arrested.

Say that you are an adult, arrested while you are out walking. You fit the description of someone the police are looking for. You face a car or a wall and spread your legs while they search your clothes for concealed weapons. Your wrists are put in handcuffs. The police officer pushes your head down as you get into the backseat of the patrol car.

It could happen on a deserted road where there is no one around but you and the police. Or it could happen on a city street where dozens of people see it. They're all thinking, "The police know what they are doing. That person committed a crime."

Now it's going to matter to you whether or not you are living in a free society. If you do, you have legal rights that can't be taken away, even if you really did commit a crime, even if powerful people are against you, even if you are accused of an act so unpopular that almost everybody wants to see you punished. You have a right not to testify against

Joseph Hunt *(right)* and his attorney Rowan K. Klein are shown here in a courtroom in April 1996 during a habeas corpus hearing. Hunt and his lawyer were appealing a 1987 murder conviction, in which Hunt was given a sentence of life in state prison without the possibility of parole. Hunt and his attorney based their habeas corpus petition on the discovery of new evidence involving the murder victim, with the hope that it would result in Hunt's being given a new trial.

yourself. You have the right not to be tortured. You have the right to know what you're accused of and to hear the evidence against you. You have the right to be represented by a lawyer who knows what your rights are and how to use them better than you do.

One of the most important of these rights is called the writ of habeas corpus. To put it into the plainest terms, habeas corpus is the legal method your lawyers can use to force the authorities to bring you to a court before a judge and to explain why they arrested you. If the judge doesn't agree with their reason, he or she makes them let you go. The right to petition for a writ of habeas corpus is so important that the Founding Fathers wrote it into the main body of the U.S. Constitution, before they added the Bill of Rights that protects other rights such as freedom of speech, the right to a trial, and the right of assembly. "The privilege of the Writ of Habeas

Corpus," the Constitution states, "shall not be suspended, unless when in Cases of Rebellion or Invasion the Public Safety May Require It."

The Founding Fathers considered habeas corpus essential because it is the right that gives citizens access to all their other rights. It says that those in power cannot ignore the law. Whatever they do, they have to do it through the courts, where other people can see that justice is done. It's the right that makes all the other rights work.

CHAPTER ONE

The History of Habeas Corpus

What is the writ of habeas corpus? The writ of habeas corpus is an order written by a judge, demanding that a prisoner be brought to the court so that the judge can decide whether the person is being lawfully imprisoned. Usually the prisoner, or someone acting in the prisoner's interests, petitions the judge to issue the writ. If the judge agrees, the prisoner will be brought to the court. Then the prosecutor and the prisoner's legal counsel argue whether the imprisonment is legal or illegal.

The writ is not the only guarantee of a prisoner's rights. Under the Constitution and its amendments no one can be imprisoned without a charge, and everyone has the right to a lawyer and to a fair trial. But the writ of habeas corpus helps make sure that people really get the rights the Constitution promises. It brings the prisoner before a judge and into a public courtroom. Even when it isn't used, a writ of habeas corpus acts as a safeguard. Prosecutors and police know that prisoners have the option of petitioning judges for a writ of habeas corpus. The police have to take it into account, so it affects the way they treat the prisoners who are in custody. Even prisoners who have already been convicted and are serving their sentence have the right to petition for a writ of habeas corpus.

HOW THE WRIT OF HABEAS CORPUS CAME TO BE

In England during the Middle Ages, law was a matter of tradition. Judges' decisions were usually shaped according to the prevailing customs, called common law. When someone was charged with a crime, or a disagreement had to be settled, authorities decided what was fair according to what had been done in earlier cases. A legal document called the writ of habeas corpus would be used by a magistrate or a sheriff to demand that someone be brought to the court. "Habeas corpus" is a Latin phrase that literally means "you may have the body."

At first, the writ of habeas corpus wasn't a way of helping prisoners. It was often used to order that people be arrested or brought from one court to another. Only over the course of centuries did the writ of habeas corpus begin to be seen as a right that helped prisoners by giving them the benefit of the law.

For that to happen, people had to develop the idea that everybody has a right to be tried according to the law. This idea entered history in 1215, when King John of England was forced to sign the Magna Carta (or "great charter").

MAGNA CARTA: EVEN THE KING IS NOT ABOVE THE LAW

John, who reigned in England from 1199 to 1216, was an unpopular king. He was disliked not only by the common people of his realm, but also by his barons, the noblemen who had soldiers at their command. In the early 1210s, when King John tried to force his barons to pay him money, they rebelled, bringing the country to the brink of civil war. To avoid bloodshed, English church officials stepped in and suggested a compromise. King John could remain at peace with his subjects if he signed a contract that set out in writing the rights of his people, rights that even he could not violate. Reluctantly King John signed this contract, which became known as the Magna Carta.

Left: This is the third version of the Magna Carta (Great Charter), which was issued in 1225, ten years after King John signed the original charter. The original Magna Carta was reissued several times later to give additional freedoms to the British people. *Right:* When King John signed the Magna Carta in 1215, he agreed to his barons' demands that he not infringe on their feudal rights. The Great Charter stood as the basis of the notion that the British people had rights that even the king must revere.

The Star Chamber

The Star Chamber was a special court used by England's kings against nobles who were too powerful to be tried in the open. The Star Chamber was named for the stars painted on the ceiling of the room where the court's meetings were held, in the Palace of Westminster in London. The meetings of this special court were secret and its decisions were final. It could order punishments of fines, prison sentences, whipping, pillorying, or branding. James I and his son Charles I used the Star Chamber to silence their opponents. The Star Chamber was abolished in 1641. Today the phrase "star chamber" is commonly invoked as a reminder that secret trials can lead to the abuse of power.

The Magna Carta said that a person could not be imprisoned, "save by lawful judgment of his peers or by the law of the land." John and the kings who came after him had to admit that even the king must obey the law of the land.

In the centuries after the Magna Carta was issued, the courts in England began using the writ of habeas corpus as a way of bringing into the court people who might have been unlawfully imprisoned. This practice gradually tied the writ of habeas corpus to the Magna Carta's protection against unlawful imprisonment.

HABEAS CORPUS IN THE STRUGGLE BETWEEN PARLIAMENT AND THE STUART KINGS

Charles Stuart, or Charles I, of England, who reigned from 1625 to 1649, was another unpopular British king. Charles, like John before him, tried to force money out of his wealthy subjects. Charles imprisoned landowners and knights who refused to "lend" him money that Charles might not repay.

Many changes had occurred between the time of King John and the time of King Charles. Over the course of centuries, starting in the late thirteenth century, England had developed a parliament, which made laws and decided what taxes would be paid to the

Charles I, king of England from 1625 to 1649, was tried for treason, convicted, and then beheaded in front of his palace of Whitehall in London. In 1628, King Charles had signed the Petition of Right, in which he agreed not to imprison his knights for refusing to pay him forced loans. The petition also restated the limits of the king's power and called his attention to his judges' refusal to reply to writs of habeas corpus.

government. When Parliament met in 1628, its members demanded that Charles sign a document like the Magna Carta, which would specify the rights of British citizens. In this document, called the Petition of Right, Parliament complained that the king's judges refused to respond to writs of habeas corpus.

Charles I signed the Petition of Right, but then he ignored it, still locking up people illegally when they got in his way. The power struggle between Parliament and the king ended with civil war. Parliament had Charles I beheaded in 1649. After a period when England was ruled by a dictatorship, the Stuart line was restored to the throne. Charles I's eldest surviving son, Charles II, was crowned

In 1689, Parliament offered the British throne to the Dutch ruler William of Orange, who is pictured here *(far right)* arriving at Torbay, on the coast of the English Channel, in 1688. Parliament, with William's support, passed a bill of rights in 1689, which restated the rights that all British citizens had, including the right to petition the king, the right of Protestant subjects to bear arms, the banning of excessive bail or fines and of cruel and unusual punishments, the right to a jury trial in cases that are punishable by death, and the right to seek changes in laws.

king. Charles II was more popular than his father, but he, too, unlawfully imprisoned his political opponents. Parliament responded by passing the Habeas Corpus Act of 1679, once more asserting citizens' rights not to be imprisoned unlawfully. Finally, Charles II's son James II so angered the English people that he had to leave the country to save his life. Parliament invited a Dutch prince, William of Orange, to become England's new king. William agreed and, with his cooperation, in 1689 Parliament passed the English Bill of Rights, laying down the liberties of British citizens.

HABEAS CORPUS IN THE CONSTITUTION

The British parliament's struggles against royal power in the 1600s were an inspiration for the British subjects who lived on the other

The Constitution of the United States (1787) is housed in the National Archives and Records Administration building in Washington, D.C. The framers of the Constitution included the right of the writ of habeas corpus in Article I, Section 9, which states, "The privilege of the Writ of Habeas Corpus shall not be suspended, unless when in Cases of Rebellion or Invasion the public Safety may require it."

side of the Atlantic Ocean, in the thirteen colonies in America. When the colonists rebelled in the 1770s, they wanted to make certain that the liberties Parliament had wrested from the kings of England applied to them as well. America's founding documents— the Declaration of Independence, the Articles of Confederation, the Constitution, and the Bill of Rights—were patterned after the great founding documents of British liberty.

The writ of habeas corpus was seen as a crucial defense against the abuse of government power. Guarantees of the writ of habeas corpus were written into several of the original thirteen states' constitutions, and into the U.S. Constitution in 1787. The Bill of Rights (the first ten amendments to the Constitution) added to the strength of the writ of habeas corpus by guaranteeing "due process of law" (Fifth Amendment), a "speedy and public trial" and "legal counsel" (Sixth Amendment), and protection against "excessive bail" (Eighth Amendment).

CHAPTER TWO
Habeas Corpus in Action

The most important purpose of a writ of habeas corpus is to force prosecutors either to charge a prisoner with a crime or to let the prisoner go free. For an American citizen to be simply locked away without a charge is fairly unusual, thanks to the mere existence of remedies like this writ. The commonest use of the writ of habeas corpus isn't to remedy such gross abuses of governmental power as locking people away without charging or trying them.

But there are more subtle ways to imprison someone unlawfully. The most common is to give a person an unfair trial. There are many ways to make a trial unfair. A trial may be unfair because the prosecutors know about evidence useful to the defense and deliberately keep it a secret. A trial may be unfair because the judge is prejudiced and lets the jury know that he or she thinks the defendant is guilty. A trial may be unfair because the police beat the prisoner to obtain a confession, or obtained evidence illegally by breaking into the defendant's house or car without a search warrant. It may be unfair because the defense lawyer is grossly incompetent and makes all kinds of mistakes that hurt the defendant's case. Or it may be that the crime is so horrifying, and makes people in the community so angry, that it is impossible to find an impartial jury in the place where the trial is being held.

Former boxer Rubin "Hurricane" Carter, who spent almost twenty years in prison after being falsely convicted of a triple murder, holds the writ of habeas corpus that freed him from prison in 1985. Carter appeared at a California news conference in 2004 to urge Governor Arnold Schwarzenegger to delay the execution of Kevin Cooper for the murder of four people in 1983. Carter said that in Cooper's case, prosecutors had withheld evidence that might prove Cooper did not commit the crime of which he had been convicted.

Finally, even after a fair trial, new evidence may turn up, such as another person confessing to the crime, that ought to entitle the defendant to a new trial.

Whether or not a trial has been unfair is a matter for a judge to decide—and of course, a different judge from the one who presided over the supposedly unfair trial must make that determination. The usual way for getting a new judge to review the fairness of a trial is by appeal, the procedure whereby the prisoner or somebody acting for the prisoner asks a higher court to look at the trial and decide if it was unfair. Every court has a higher court over it, except for the

U.S. Supreme Court, which sits at the top of the ladder. Higher courts exist for the special purpose of reviewing the decisions of lower courts. Usually, the highest court in each state is that state's supreme court, although in some states, the highest court is called by another title; for example, New York's is called the court of appeals. If the state supreme court upholds the conviction, or refuses to hear the case, the prisoner can petition a federal–that is, United States–court to issue a writ of habeas corpus to bring the prisoner to federal court and review the case. Prisoners who believe their constitutional rights have been violated can even petition the U.S. Supreme Court, the highest court in the nation, for a writ of habeas corpus.

A judge will issue a writ of habeas corpus only if he or she is convinced that a prisoner hasn't received a fair shake from the regular appeals process.

HABEAS CORPUS IN DEATH PENALTY CASES

One of the best-known modern uses of the writ of habeas corpus involves prisoners who are sentenced to death for their conviction in serious crimes, such as murder, kidnapping, and hijacking of aircraft. Starting in the middle of the twentieth century, it became a matter of routine for such prisoners to file multiple petitions for writs of habeas corpus to ask for review by a federal court, which has the power to review state court decisions that may violate the Constitution. The lawyers for a death row inmate would often file a petition for a writ of habeas corpus at the last minute–shortly before the prisoner was about to be executed–on constitutional grounds or on the grounds that important new evidence had come to light. The court would order that the execution be put off so that it had time to review the petition.

In this way, the execution would be put off again and again. During the early 1960s, late 1970s, and 1980s, defense lawyers often used these multiple writs of habeas corpus as a delaying tactic, hoping

THE WRIT OF HABEAS CORPUS

On April 15, 2003, Texas state senators Rodney Ellis *(left)* and Chris Harris met during a Senate session in Austin to discuss a new law that would see to it that lawyers assigned to handle death row habeas corpus cases are competent to do their job. On the following day, the Texas Senate passed the bill, SB 1224, which was designed to ensure that Texas death row inmates are given one full and fair chance to have their habeas corpus and unfairness claims heard by the courts.

to put off the execution for years (perhaps until the country changed its mind about the use of capital punishment, or the death penalty). A 1991 decision by the U.S. Supreme Court changed the rules to make it much harder for prisoners to obtain more than one writ of habeas corpus.

HABEAS CORPUS IN BAD PRISON CONDITIONS

The Eighth Amendment of the Constitution states that citizens of the United States may not be subjected to "cruel and unusual punishment." In prison, living conditions may be so bad that spending time in them amounts to cruel and unusual punishment.

Even the average prison is a dangerous place, where weaker inmates are prey to the stronger. Some prisons, however, might be worse than others. They might be overcrowded, because a state could be locking up more people than it has room to hold. They might provide substandard food, because prison officials could be corrupt or because the state might be too stingy to give the prison money to feed its inmates adequately. They might use unnecessarily harsh punishments. When these abuses occur, they can be grounds for getting a judge to file a writ of habeas corpus.

HABEAS CORPUS FOR INMATES IN MENTAL INSTITUTIONS

Prisons are not the only places where people are kept under lock and key. Mental patients who are considered to be a danger to themselves and others are also restrained. Instead of cells with bars and prison guards, there are hospital beds, recreation rooms, and a nursing staff dispensing powerful drugs in paper cups. The inmates of mental hospitals include private patients who commit themselves for treatment or are committed by their relatives. Also in mental hospitals are people who have committed crimes but have been deemed not guilty by reason of insanity, and offenders who have accepted treatment in a mental hospital as an alternative to time in prison. Inmates in mental hospitals may not leave until an expert decides that they are no longer dangerous—which might turn out to be never.

Providing treatment instead of punishment for people who are dangerous because of mental illness is probably the right thing to do, but it's an approach that can be abused. In the Soviet Union before its breakup in 1991, the state locked up its political opponents in mental hospitals under the guise of treating them. While the U.S.

At an Arkansas detention center, a prisoner looks out the grated door as he breathes in fresh air in May 2004. The sheriff of the Arkansas county where the center is located announced that at least twenty inmates would be released early because of the center's overcrowded conditions. In certain cases, overcrowding at institutions such as this might be grounds for cruel and unusual punishment, and, hence, grounds for obtaining a writ of habeas corpus.

Habeas Corpus and Slavery

Before the Civil War (1861–1865), abolitionists used the writ of habeas corpus to win freedom for slaves who had escaped to free states. The Fugitive Slave Act of 1850 said that escaped slaves had to be sent back to the slaveholders. Abolitionists used legal tricks to thwart this law. When a slave was found in the North, an antislavery lawyer would file a writ of habeas corpus to bring the case before a Northern jury, whose members would be likely to let the slave go free. However, slaveholders also used writs to order that sheriffs bring them their "property."

government has never used mental hospitals that way, mental patients still face the problem of being forgotten by the outside world. For these patients, habeas corpus is a valuable resource. The law permits them to file a petition for a writ of habeas corpus to challenge the basis for continuing their confinement.

HABEAS CORPUS IN IMMIGRATION LAW

Writs of habeas corpus are not just available to citizens of the United States, but to immigrants as well, because even noncitizens are not outside the law. When the government charges that immigrants have committed crimes, or when it is believed that they committed crimes in the country from which they came, U.S. law enforcement agencies may decide to deport them, that is, to send them back to their country of origin. Immigrants can challenge the legality of this decision by petitioning federal courts for a writ of habeas corpus.

HABEAS CORPUS IN FAMILY COURT

When parents are divorced, the parents may go to family court to help settle disputes about their children, especially which parent the children should reside with, and how often the children can visit the other parent. A writ of habeas corpus may be issued if there's a sudden change in the situation. For example, the parent with whom the children live may move out of the state, so the other parent can no longer visit the children. Or one parent may believe that the other parent has become unfit to take care of the children. In these cases and others, parents may petition the court for a writ of habeas corpus. The writ will cause the children to be brought into family court where the judge will make decisions based on their best interest.

CHAPTER THREE

Habeas Corpus Suspended

Few Americans have ever done more for the cause of freedom than Abraham Lincoln. As president and commander in chief, Lincoln won the Civil War. He kept the United States intact. He freed the slaves. Lincoln's accomplishments led, after his death, to the passage of the Thirteenth Amendment (1865), which outlawed slavery, and of the Fourteenth Amendment (1868), which prevents states from depriving citizens of life or liberty without due process of law. As later interpreted by the U.S. Supreme Court, the Fourteenth Amendment saw to it that state laws have to give citizens the same civil liberties that U.S. laws give them. Civil libertarians owe a lot to Lincoln.

Yet no American president ever did as much as Abraham Lincoln did to restrict civil liberties when he was in office. Under Lincoln's authority, thousands of American citizens were thrown into jail without trials. By Lincoln's command, several thousand civilians were tried by military commission in places where civilian courts were open—in other words, they were denied the constitutional right to trial by a jury of their peers. Lincoln put his signature to nine orders and proclamations that formally announced the suspension of the writ of habeas corpus in 1861. When Roger B. Taney, chief justice of the Supreme Court, wrote an opinion that Lincoln was acting illegally under the

President Abraham Lincoln *(second from right)*, who appears in this photo with General George McClellan *(second from left)* at Antietam in 1862, suspended the writ of habeas corpus on several occasions during the American Civil War (1861–1865).

Constitution, Lincoln ignored it and even considered arresting Taney. At the time, many people, not all of them Southerners, considered Lincoln a tyrant, but because there was a war going on, there was little they could do about it.

THE EMERGENCY

On the other hand, few Americans would deny that the circumstances in the early 1860s were unusual. When he took the oath of office in March 1861, Lincoln faced a situation unlike any other in American history before or since. In February, seven states had left the Union. They had formed the Confederate States of America and had begun occupying federal buildings, post offices, forts, and other U.S. government property. By the end of May, another four states would leave the Union and join the Confederacy. Of the states in which slavery was legal, only four–the border states of Delaware, Maryland, Kentucky, and Missouri–were still in the Union. As he prepared for a war to save the Union, Lincoln had every reason to believe that if he did not act quickly, the border states would leave as well. If that happened, keeping the United States intact might be impossible.

Washington, D.C., the nation's capital, lay wedged between two slave states. Virginia, to the south of Washington, had already joined the Confederacy; Maryland, to the north, was still undecided. On April 14, 1861, news arrived in Washington that the Confederates had fired on Fort Sumter. The war had begun. On April 19, soldiers from Massachusetts, on the way to guard Washington, were blocked by a mob of people who wanted Maryland to leave the Union. For several days no one in Washington knew if soldiers would be able to come to defend the capital. Even after they arrived, Lincoln's general in chief Winfield Scott told him that there was a good chance Washington might be attacked and that the bridges leading into the city were in danger.

Roger B. Taney served as chief justice of the U.S. Supreme Court when President Abraham Lincoln suspended the writ of habeas corpus. Taney believed that the Constitution gave the power to suspend the writ of habeas corpus only to Congress and that the president had no authority to take this step on his own.

On April 27, Lincoln gave an order suspending the writ of habeas corpus "at any point on or in the vicinity of any military line, which is now or which shall be used within the City of Philadelphia and the City of Washington."

Lincoln later expanded his suspension of the writ of habeas corpus to include most of the country. Lincoln gave the power to make arrests to military commanders, who often arrested people Lincoln would probably have left alone. People were imprisoned for many different reasons. Some had been actively working for the Confederacy as irregular fighters. Others were citizens of Confederate

POLITICAL CARICATURE Nº 1.

This political cartoon, entitled *The Grave of the Union, Or Major Jack Downing's Dream*, was published in New York in 1864. In its harsh anti-Lincoln stance, an imaginary dream of Jack Downing, a Yankee character created in the 1830s, has portrayed Lincoln and some of his supporters and cabinet members as a band of undertakers who are about to inter the U.S. Constitution.

states who happened to be stranded in the North at the start of the Civil War, and might be spies, though it could not be proven that they were. Some were Northerners who opposed the war. Some were draft resisters. Some were arrested merely for the words they spoke, urging soldiers to desert, criticizing Lincoln's policies, and, in a couple of cases, merely saying harsh words about Lincoln. In one case a minister who refused to pray for the president was arrested and denied the writ of habeas corpus.

Lincoln was not a vain man, and he knew that arrests for people who spoke ill of him personally were bad policy. They made him look like a tyrant and angered many people who would otherwise have supported him. He also knew that it was unwise to arrest newspaper editors merely for criticizing the war, and for the most part he left such people alone. But when overzealous generals under him went too far and arrested people for disloyalty, he still backed up their decisions.

Lincoln's main legal justification for suspending habeas corpus was the Constitution, which stated that the writ of habeas corpus could not be suspended "except in case of insurrection or invasion." Clearly Lincoln did face an insurrection. However, the words about the suspension of habeas corpus were in Article I of the Constitution, where the powers given to Congress are discussed, not in Article II, which lays out the powers of the presidency. Because of this, Chief Justice Roger Taney did not think the president had the right to suspend the writ of habeas corpus. He issued a writ of habeas corpus to one of the men arrested under Lincoln's orders. When Chief Justice Taney's writ was ignored, Taney wrote a Supreme Court opinion stating that Lincoln was exceeding his authority as president.

Scholars still debate Lincoln's decision to suspend the writ of habeas corpus. In the hands of a genuinely power-hungry president, Lincoln's actions would have been dangerous. It happened that Lincoln's instincts were democratic. Lincoln did not use his extraordinary wartime powers to stifle debate. Throughout the war, newspapers in the North published attacks on Lincoln and his party, and a fair and open presidential election was held in the midst of the Civil War.

INTERNMENT OF JAPANESE AMERICANS IN THE SECOND WORLD WAR

American citizens were again interned without charge or trial during the Second World War (1939–1945). On December 7, 1941, the

Japanese Americans are pictured here waiting for directions during their internment in August 1942 at Puyallup Assembly Center, called Camp Harmony, in the state of Washington. Japanese Americans were forced to leave their homes, sell their possessions, and move into the internment camps after President Franklin D. Roosevelt's Executive Order 9066, which took effect after the U.S. government declared war on Japan and its allies.

Every year the human rights group Amnesty International publishes a report of the state of human rights around the world. According to Amnesty International's 2004 report, executions without a trial were carried out in forty-seven countries in 2003. In twenty-eight countries, governments made people disappear (that is, people were arrested or kidnapped and no information was provided about their fate). People were arbitrarily arrested and detained without charge or trial in fifty-eight countries.

American naval base at Pearl Harbor in Hawaii was attacked by Japanese forces. Japanese spies on the Hawaiian island of Oahu had assisted in preparations for the attack. Fearing an attack on the West Coast of the United States, American war planners became suspicious of Japanese Americans in California, Oregon, and Washington. On Executive Order 9066, from President Franklin D. Roosevelt, beginning in early 1942, more than 100,000 people of Japanese origin were forcibly relocated to camps in the interior of California, Arizona, Utah, Idaho, Colorado, and Wyoming and held there for most of the war. Unlike Lincoln, Roosevelt never officially suspended the writ of habeas corpus, but the effect on Japanese Americans was the same as if he had.

Some of those moved from their homes were not U.S. citizens; others were American citizens of Japanese descent. Some Asians of non-Japanese origin were relocated as well. The U.S. Supreme Court decided afterward that the president had acted within his powers in ordering the relocation. Historians have come to regard both the internment and the Supreme Court decisions as serious mistakes.

LIBERTY IN WARTIME

Both the Civil War and the Second World War offer a lesson on the danger that wars pose for human rights, regardless of the justice of the particular war. War puts great pressure on civil liberties. During wartime, anyone can come under suspicion as an enemy agent. People who disagree with wartime leaders may be branded as traitors. In wartime, governments are quick to claim extraordinary powers.

Yet civil liberties are never so important as they are in wartime. The people who fight in the war and send their children to fight in the war need to be able to discuss the wisdom of the war. They need to discuss the effectiveness of the methods used to conduct it. They can't give their leaders the right to be above criticism just because the country is at war.

CHAPTER FOUR

Habeas Corpus Under Stress

Americans look to the U.S. Supreme Court when they want to find out if a new law or a government action violates the U.S. Constitution. The Supreme Court decides the difficult cases in which it is not clear how the law applies. Judges across the country use the Supreme Court as a guide, so the decisions of the Supreme Court affect what happens in local police stations and courtrooms throughout the nation.

The justices of the Supreme Court are not infallible, however. They are products of their time, and in different eras they have tended to interpret the Constitution differently. In the early 1800s, they saw the Constitution as a defender of the rights of states against the federal government. In the late 1800s and early 1900s, the Supreme Court saw the Constitution as the protector of corporations against government interference. In the middle of the 1900s, the Supreme Court paid special attention to the parts of the Constitution that protected civil liberties.

Earlier judges had not ignored civil liberties, but from the 1930s through the 1960s, the Supreme Court placed more emphasis on them than ever before. The Court bent over backward to defend the rights of the accused. It forced police in all states to inform arrested people of their right not to testify against themselves and their right to have a lawyer. It told police they

Dangerous Precedents Occur in Dangerous Times

During the 1807 *United States v. Bollman* case, William Cranch, who was judge of the Circuit Court of the District of Columbia, wrote about the duty of judges to protect the rule of law in times of crisis.

"When the public mind is agitated, when wars, and rumors of war, plots, conspiracies and treasons excite or alarm, it is the duty of the court to be particularly watchful . . . In the calm of peace and prosperity, there is seldom great injustice. Dangerous precedents occur in dangerous times. It then becomes the duty of the judiciary calmly to pose the scales of justice, unmoved by the arm of power, undisturbed by the clamor of the multitude."

had to get a warrant before they could tap someone's phone. It ruled that if the police obtained evidence during an illegal search, the evidence couldn't be used in court, even if not using it meant letting a guilty person go free. The Supreme Court made many other decisions that defended individual rights.

THE ERA OF EXPANDING CIVIL LIBERTIES ENDS

In the 1970s and 1980s, this era of expanding liberty gradually came to an end. There were many reasons for this change. One was a sharp rise in crime. All over the country, during the 1970s and 1980s, the media were filled with stories of drug addiction, murders, and muggings. People felt less safe walking the streets of the cities. Many people accused the courts of giving criminals free reign by making it too hard for the police to gather evidence and get confessions. Some of the same people were angry about other Supreme Court decisions, which legalized abortion, prevented Congress from passing a law to jail protesters who burned the U.S. flag, and forced Southern states to end racial segregation.

As a result, U.S. presidents were elected (Richard Nixon, Ronald Reagan, George H. W. Bush) who promised to appoint Supreme Court justices who would not find any new rights in the

Constitution. These presidents fulfilled their campaign promises, appointing Supreme Court justices who took a narrower view of constitutional liberties. As the liberal justices died or retired, conservative justices became the majority. The era in which the Supreme Court expanded the rights of the accused was over.

HABEAS CORPUS AND THE DEATH PENALTY

The new Supreme Court decided to make it easier for states to execute prisoners who had been convicted and sentenced to death. For years during the 1950s and 1960s, defenders of those sentenced to die had used every legal trick they could to postpone their clients' executions. A favorite method was to petition the courts for many writs of habeas corpus, each putting forward a new reason that the case needed to be reviewed. Clearly this was often done as a delaying tactic. However, such petitions sometimes led to findings that death row prisoners had been wrongfully convicted, so the earlier, more liberal Court had been reluctant to limit them. The new Court had no such reluctance. In a case decided in 1991, *McClesky v. Zant*, the Court made it much more difficult for death row inmates to petition for a second writ of habeas corpus.

In 1996, Congress passed the Anti-Terrorism and Effective Death Penalty Act, which further limited death row inmates' use of habeas corpus petitions. According to the 1996 law, federal courts may order new trials only if they find that state courts were not merely incorrect but "unreasonable" in making their decision. The U.S. Supreme Court later ruled that the Anti-Terrorism and Effective Death Penalty Act did not violate the Constitution.

HABEAS CORPUS AFTER 9/11

On September 11, 2001, terrorists attacked the United States, hijacking commercial jets and flying them into the World Trade

U.S. senator Orrin Hatch addresses reporters outside the U.S. Supreme Court building in Washington, D.C., in June 1996. As chairman of the Senate Judiciary Committee, Hatch gave the news media an update after a hearing about a new law limiting federal appeals by death row inmates. Many lawmakers complained that death row inmates' appeals could delay executions for ten years or more.

The New York City skyline fills with smoke after terrorists attacked the World Trade Center towers on September 11, 2001. The U.S. government has since declared war on terrorism and has worked to pass legislation that protects its citizens' rights while capturing suspected terrorists who aim to commit crimes against U.S. citizens.

Center in New York City, the Pentagon near Washington, D.C., and a field in Pennsylvania. Thousands of innocent people were killed in the terrorist attacks. It was the worst assault on U.S. soil since the Japanese strike on Pearl Harbor in 1941. A mood of crisis fell over the country. Americans turned to their leaders, eager to cooperate in any action the government might take against this ruthless enemy.

Determining that the terrorist group Al Qaeda was responsible for the attack, in January 2002, the United States invaded Afghanistan, where Al Qaeda had its base of operations. In the

Inside a holding area at the U.S. Naval Base Guantánamo Bay's Camp X-Ray, naval military police guard the first detainees from Afghanistan in January 2002. Most of the detainees are accused by the U.S. government of being either Taliban soldiers or Al Qaeda terrorist operatives. According to President George W. Bush, the prisoners held there are not subject to the laws of the United States, which allow writs of habeas corpus to be filed even for aliens.

course of the war in Afghanistan, the United States captured 660 suspected terrorists from about forty countries and transported them to the U.S. Naval Base in Guantánamo Bay, Cuba. Guantánamo Bay was chosen as the place to detain these men because it is under the control of the United States but technically is not in U.S. territory. Therefore, according to President George W. Bush, the prisoners held there are not subject to the laws of the United States, which allow writs of habeas corpus to be filed even for aliens.

Two years passed as the men captured in Afghanistan were held in Guantánamo Bay without access to lawyers or family. The military questioned the prisoners, using methods that were unusually harsh. According to a report released by the International Committee of the Red Cross in November 2004, some of these methods amount to torture. The government of the United States denies the Red Cross's charges, and at the time of this writing it is difficult to know for sure, because everything done to the prisoners is shrouded in secrecy. The government said that the interrogations had yielded information important to the war on terror. Critics of the Bush administration said that the president was setting a dangerous precedent. The men held at Guantánamo Bay might or might not be terrorists, but by denying them access to any legal review the government was violating both U.S. and international law.

The United States also denied the protections of law to Yaser Hamdi and Joseph Padilla, two U.S. citizens captured in connection with the war on terror. In late June 2004, the cases of Hamdi, Padilla, and several Guantánamo Bay prisoners were decided by the U.S. Supreme Court in two separate cases, in which two similar lawsuits were joined as one case because the legal issues at stake were closely related. In decisions concerning the prisoners Hamdi and Padilla, the Supreme Court ruled that the president does have authority to order U.S. citizens to be held without charge or trial, but that detainees can challenge their treatment in U.S. courts. "A state

Left: U.S.-born Yaser Esam Hamdi is led away by a Northern Alliance soldier on an Afghanistan battlefield in December 2001. Hamdi was sent to the Guantánamo Bay detention center, where he awaited charges. *Right:* Frank Dunham, attorney for Yaser Hamdi, speaks to reporters outside the U.S. Supreme Court building in Washington, D.C., in April 2004. Dunham argued before the Court that the president had overstepped his authority by imprisoning American citizens suspected of terrorism and denying them access to lawyers and courts.

of war is not a blank check for the President," Justice Sandra Day O'Connor wrote in her opinion regarding Hamdi. In two other cases, *Al Odah v. United States* and *Rasul v. Bush,* the Supreme Court ruled that the government was wrong to maintain that Guantánamo Bay was beyond the reach of U.S. law. As of June 2004, it looked as though the prisoners would have their day in court. Time will tell how this historic Supreme Court ruling affects the future of suspected terrorists.

PROTECTING OTHER PEOPLE'S RIGHTS TO PROTECT OUR OWN

Words on paper have done a great deal to guarantee human rights, but they have never done it alone. Rights such as the right to file a writ of habeas corpus are rooted in custom and history. They were built up very gradually over hundreds of years. They were made into a practical reality by means of countless small victories. Every time a right is enforced, it becomes stronger for all of us.

Just as rights are won by many small victories, they can be lost by means of many tiny defeats. Every time a right is violated in the name of expediency, it becomes weaker for all of us.

Above all, the strength of our rights depends on the attitude of the people. We all get angry when we think our own rights are being violated, but do we object when we see somebody else's rights violated? We may shrug and say, "Well, it may not be legal, but it's fair. He deserved it." This course of action is neither patriotic nor wise. The way a right is enforced today is the most important guarantee that the right will continue to exist in the future.

GLOSSARY

abolitionist One who opposes slavery and wants to abolish it.

Al Qaeda An Arabic word meaning "the foundation." Al Qaeda is an independent military organization that is heavily influenced by its interpretation of the Islamic religion. Established by Osama bin Laden in 1988, it is widely regarded as a terrorist organization.

appeal A legal proceeding by which a case is brought before a higher court to review the decision of a lower court.

bail Temporary release of a prisoner, usually in exchange for an amount of money to be held as an assurance that the prisoner will return for his or her trial. Also, the amount of money that the prisoner has to put up in order to be released.

Bill of Rights A summary of fundamental rights guaranteed to people against violation by the state. The first ten amendments of the U.S. Constitution are commonly referred to as the Bill of Rights.

circuit court A general trial court, sometimes called a district court or a superior court. The judges go on "circuit" from one county to another according to a schedule.

civil liberties Freedom from the abuse of government power, especially the protections guaranteed by the U.S. Constitution and its amendments.

custody Immediate charge and control (as over a child or a prisoner) exercised by a person or an authority.

death row A prison area housing inmates who have been convicted and sentenced to die.

detainee A person held in custody; a prisoner.

due process Legal proceedings carried out in accordance with established rules and principles.

federal Having to do with the national, rather than state or local, government.

inmate A person confined, such as a prisoner or a hospital patient.

interrogation Formal, systematic questioning.

magistrate An official entrusted with the administration of the law. In the Middle Ages, magistrates combined the functions of law enforcement and judge.

precedent In law, a judge's decision that may act as a rule or model to guide the decisions of other judges in similar circumstances.

sheriff The head law enforcement official of a shire or county. In the Middle Ages, sheriffs combined the functions of judge and law enforcement officer.

terrorism Commonly used term referring to the calculated use of violence or the threat of violence against a civilian population for the purpose of producing fear, usually for some political end.

warrant A document issued usually by a judge, giving police authority to do something such as make an arrest, seize property, or conduct a search.

FOR MORE INFORMATION

American Civil Liberties Union
125 Broad Street, 18th Floor
New York, NY 10004
(212) 549-2500
Web site: http://www.aclu.org

Amnesty International USA
5 Penn Plaza, 14th Floor
New York, NY 10001
(212) 807-8400
Web site: http://www.amnestyusa.org

National Constitution Center
525 Arch Street, Independence Mall
Philadelphia, PA 19106
(215) 409-6600
Web site: http://www.constitutioncenter.org/index.shtml

Web Sites

Due to the changing nature of Internet links, the Rosen Publishing Group, Inc., has developed an online list of Web sites related to the subject of this book. This site is updated regularly. Please use this link to access the list:

http://www.rosenlinks.com/lallp/wrhc

FOR FURTHER READING

Burgan, Michael. *The Bill of Rights*. Minneapolis, MN: Compass Point Books, 2002.

Farish, Leah. *The First Amendment: Freedom of Speech, Religion, and the Press*. Berkeley Heights, NJ: Enslow, 1998.

Johnson, Linda Carlson. *Our Constitution*. Brookfield, CT: The Millbrook Press, 1992.

Krull, Kathleen. *Kids' Guide to America's Bill of Rights: Curfews, Censorship, and the 100-Pound Giant*. New York, NY: HarperCollins, 1999.

Lindop, Edmund. *The Bill of Rights and Landmark Cases*. New York, NY: Franklin Watts, 1989.

Patrick, John J. *The Supreme Court of the United States: A Student Companion*. New York, NY: Oxford University Press, 2002.

Scheppler, Bill. *Guantánamo Bay and Military Tribunals: The Detention and Trial of Suspected Terrorists* (Frontline Coverage of Current Events). New York, NY: The Rosen Publishing Group, Inc., 2005.

Sobel, Syl, and Denise Gilgannon. *The U.S. Constitution and You*. Hauppauge, NY: Barrons Educational Series, 2001.

Stein, R. Conrad. *The Powers of the Supreme Court*. Chicago, IL: Children's Press, 1995.

BIBLIOGRAPHY

Abernathy, M. Glenn. *Civil Liberties Under the Constitution.* New York, NY: Dodd, Mead & Company, 1968.

Fraenkel, Osmond K. *The Rights We Have.* New York, NY: Thomas & Crowell Company, 1971.

Levy, Leonard W. *Origins of the Bill of Rights.* New Haven, CT: Yale University Press, 1999.

Neely, Mark E., Jr. *The Fate of Liberty: Abraham Lincoln and Civil Liberties.* New York, NY: Oxford University Press, 1991.

O'Brien, David M. *Constitutional Law and Politics.* New York, NY: W. W. Norton & Company, 2000.

Rehnquist, William H. *All the Laws but One: Civil Liberties in Wartime.* New York, NY: Alfred A. Knopf, 1998.

Sutherland, Arthur E. *Constitutionalism in America: Origin and Evolution of Its Fundamental Ideas.* New York, NY: Blaisdell Publishing Company, 1965.

INDEX

About the Author

Phillip Margulies has a keen interest in American history and the constitutional roots of American democracy. He is the author of many nonfiction books for children and young adults. He is the editor of several history anthologies. Margulies, who lives in New York City, is the recipient of the New York Foundation for the Arts Fellowships for both nonfiction and fiction.

Photo Credits

Cover, p. 1 © Royalty Free/Corbis; pp. 5, 16, 18, 20, 35, 37, 39 (right) © AP/Wide World Photo; pp. 9, 11, 12, 24 Bettmann/Corbis; p. 9 (inset) Alecto Historical Editions, London, UK/Bridgeman Art Library; p. 13 courtesy NARA; pp. 26, 27 © Library of Congress, Prints and Photographs Division; p. 29 © *Seattle Post-Intelligencer* Collection, Museum of History and Industry/Corbis; p. 36 © Robert Essel NYC/Corbis; p. 39 (left) © Reuters/Corbis.

Designer: Thomas Forget; Editor: Kathy Kuhtz Campbell